A Basic Confucius

An Introduction to the Wisdom and Advice of
China's Greatest Sage

Compiled by Kuijie Zhou

LONG RIVER PRESS

First Edition 2005
Copyright © 2005 Long River Press
Editors: Luo Tianyou, Sun Lei
All rights reserved
No part of this book may be reproduced without written
permission of the publisher

Library of Congress Cataloging-in-Publication Data

Zhou, Kuijie.

A basic Confucius : an introduction to the wisdom and advice of China's
greatest sage / compiled by Kuijie Zhou.
       p. cm.
  ISBN 1-59265-040-6 (hardcover)
  1. Philosophy, Confucian. 2. Confucius. I. Title.
B127.C65Z48 2005
181'.112--dc22

                              2004023416

A Basic Confucius
Published in the United States of America by
Long River Press
360 Swift Avenue, Suite 48
South San Francisco, CA 94080
www.longriverpress.com

Printed in China
10 9 8 7 6 5 4 3 2 1

Contents

Introduction

Confucius is perhaps the greatest philosopher in Chinese history, and is also one of the most studied philosophers in the history of human civilization. The body of writings which comprise his teachings and interpretations have been handed down for generations and have guided and influenced nearly every aspect of Chinese society for thousands of years. Arguably, the teachings of Confucius have had the single greatest impact on Chinese history, more than any other social or historical factor.

Confucius was born around 550 B.C. in the State of Lu, which was located in today's Shandong province. Like many Chinese in his time, Confucius had political aspirations. China was divided, both geographically and philosophically. Various states and regions vied for political and social control. Alliances were made and then broken. Wars were waged. This period, collectively known as the Spring and Autumn and Warring States periods(c.770-221 B.C), gave rise to many different schools of philosophical and cultural thought, such as the Daoist writings of *Lao Zi* (*Lao Tzu*) and *Zhuang Zi* (*Chuang Tzu*), as well as the military treatises of philosophers like *Sunzi* (*Sun Tzu*).

Simply put, Confucian thought affected every aspect of Chinese life and how every aspect of life related directly to a series of highly structured—but rigid—relationships. Distilled down to its basic elements, it is a guide to moral values and proper social conduct. It was the responsibility of the ruler to be just and of high moral character, which would in turn enable the people to follow his example.

Confucius advocated the idea of reciprocity and responsible rule. Indeed, the paradigm of Confucian thought is that one should not do to others what one dislikes oneself. This is not unlike the concept of karma. With this idea came the advocacy of benevolent rule: the idea that if the ruler, or sage, was just in his use of power, the people would follow; if not, he would be overthrown.

Not surprisingly, given the social milieu of the time, few

rulers found the ideas of Confucius of any practical use in their attempt to grasp what power they could. Confucius ultimately failed to attain a political position of any significance. His life, on the surface, resembled failure, yet he resolved to wander about, attracting loyal disciples in the process. For 14 years he traveled throughout China. While he was usually received with polite indifference by local rulers, his views were not taken seriously or were dismissed altogether. One such ruler likened him to a stray dog looking for a home, and Confucius did not deny the similarity.

When Confucius died around 479 B.C., his ideas were not universally known and the idea of Confucian thought as a true "philosophy" had not taken root. His teachings were recorded and compiled by many generations of disciples and are now known as the "Four Books," the essential texts which form the basis of Confucian thought. They are: *The Analects, The Great Learning, The Doctrine of the Mean,* and *The Book of Mencius.*

Confucianism has falsely been labeled as a religion. In reality it was a system of thoughts and social rites and was primarily concerned with the needs of Chinese society and its societal relationships. Unlike Buddhism or Taoism, Confucianism made no provisions with dealing with the afterlife or the role of nature.

In the midst of political and social uncertainty, Confucian thought advocated five basic properties: benevolence, righteousness, propriety, wisdom, and trustworthiness. Among them, benevolence was considered as the cornerstone, encompassing faithfulness, filial piety, tolerance and kindness. By maintaining good harmony, a civilization ruled by a standardized and universally-understood system of manners, represented the ethos of Confucian-based government.

Historically speaking, Confucian thought contained many paradoxes, and would fall in and out of favor with the rise and fall of the Chinese dynasties. Confucian thought was also considered dangerous, and rulers lived in fear that the people would rise up against them. The first emperor of China, Qin Shi Huang, ever fearful of rebellion, ordered the destruction of Confucian texts and the execution of Confucian scholars. Confucius was against tyranny and oppression while at the same time he espoused that the ruling class held superiority which was inviolate. He further prescribed that the wife must be completely devoted to the husband; the son to the father, and the student to the teacher. Originally, these relationships clearly delineated "superior" vs. "inferior" characteristics. Even when one substitutes "dominant" for "subordinate," one is still left puzzled. Rather than concentrate on different "classes" of society, however, the most important elements derived from Confucian thought simply promote cultivation of the individual, irrespective of historical contexts.

Most of the sayings and teachings of Confucius were collected and complied by his disciples and form the basis of *The Analects,* which later became the textbook for future generations of disciples. The stories of the wisdom of Confucius which make up this volume are included for the benefit of those new to Confucian thought: they represent both the basic philosophical foundations of Chinese society, as well as offering profound, yet subtle lessons for individual cultivation and further study.

CHAPTER ONE

On Self-Cultivation

Do not impose on others what you yourself dislike.

This is known as the "Golden Mean" of Confucian thought. Confucius' disciple, Zhong Gong, once asked what benevolence was. Confucius answered: "Do your work as earnestly and conscientiously as you would receive a distinguished guest; summon people to perform manual labor as if you were attending a sacred ceremony; and never impose upon others what you don't wish upon yourself. By doing so you will not incur resentment."

A true gentleman is always open-minded while a petty man is always anxious.

Empress Wu Zetian (624-705 AD) had heard from one of her courtiers that one of her subjects, named Di Renjie, was kind-hearted and honest. Empress Wu wanted to know the truth for herself. She therefore asked Di if he would like to know who it was who spoke ill of him behind his back? Di answered calmly: "If I have done anything wrong, I would like to put it right. But I have no interest in knowing who may have spoken unpleasant things about me with Your Majesty."

When you meet a man of virtue, try to be as virtuous as him; when you meet a man without virtue, examine yourself to see if you have the same defects.

During the Spring and Autumn Period (772-481 BC) a man named Zi went to visit his friend Prince Cheng. The prince served him a dish made from salamander meat. Zi said, "I do not believe that gentlemen eat salamander." The prince then asked, "Are you a gentleman?" Zi answered: "The gentleman always studies in an effort to improve his moral integrity. If one only follows without improving, one's morality will deteriorate. This is the root of evil-doing. How dare I think I am a gentleman? I merely have the desire to *become* a gentleman."

Orchids in remote places may look and smell beautiful, though no one sees, smell, or admires them.

Confucius was caught in a siege being laid against the states of Chen and Cai, and for many days was without food. All his disciples were similarly starved. Zi Lu, a disciple, asked: "Master, you do good work every day, yet why do you still suffer such ill fate?" Confucius said: "When one has talent but not opportunity, one's talent cannot be put into good use. Once the opportunity comes, is there any more difficulty?" He further explained: "The one that is talented but is not given the opportunity is like the orchid deep in thick forests and remote valleys: although it never stops emanating a wondrous fragrance, no one can admire it.

Wealth and high rank are like fleeting clouds.

Confucius was engaged in a discussion with his disciples on the meaning of happiness. Some thought an affluent life represented the meaning of happiness, while some believed high social status was the meaning of happiness. Confucius had a different opinion. He said: "In my view, happiness lies in eating coarse food, drinking cold water, and sleeping with my head resting on my arm. Wealth and high rank are nothing more than clouds fleeting by."

Poor but not adulatory. Rich but not haughty.

During the Warring States Period (481-468 BC), Xinling Jun, a nobleman of the State of Wei, enjoyed high rank and great wealth, but was in no way overbearing in his demeanor. There was also a wise old man named Hou Ying, who worked as gatekeeper in the Wei capital. News of Hou Ying's wisdom eventually reached Xinling Jun. Xinling Jun then drove a carriage personally to meet with Hou Ying. Xinling Jun and Hou Ying later visited Hou's friend, and Xinling Jun, nobleman that he was, waited patiently while Hou Ying and his friend engaged in their own conversation. Hou Ying was taken aback by Xinling Jun's modesty and sincerity, and thereafter assisted Xinling Jun wholeheartedly.

B laming others' faults cannot glorify oneself; blaming others' bad conduct cannot ensure one's own proper conduct.

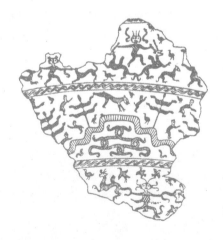

During the Spring and Autumn Period, Shusun Wushu, a senior official of the State of Lu, visited another official named Yan Hui, who duly received him with courtesy. Shusun Wushu was keen on finding others' faults and making frivolous remarks. Yan Hui could see this and in turn gave Shusun Wushu this advice: "If you continue to do this, you will bring nothing but blame to yourself. My teacher Confucius has ever said that blaming others for their faults cannot glorify oneself, and blaming others for their bad conduct cannot ensure one's own proper conduct. A true gentleman should comment on one's own short-comings rather than those of others."

Say yes when you really know. Say no when you don't. This is the way to become a wise person.

Confucius' disciple, Zi Lu, visited Confucius one day dressed in fine clothes. Confucius asked him: "What are you going to do by wearing such fine clothes? When the river passes Minshan Mountain, it is thin and slow. But at the section in Jiangjin it is so torrential that boats have to be bound together to cross it. Isn't this because of the confluence of water in the lower reaches? How do people dare give you any advice when you are clad in such brilliant clothes?" On hearing this, Zi Lu hurried home to change his clothes. Confucius said: "You must remember: those who boast are superficial. Only a petty man is conceited and contemptuous of others. A gentleman should know that he can talk of only what he understands and do only what he is capable of doing. It is wise to speak truly, and it is benevolent to behave properly. What can't you learn when you are wise and benevolent?"

夫子之道中恕而已矣意 告仁以吾道可中已所不欲物施於仁曰恕乎 子曰君子

小仁喻於利 喻猶曉也 子曰見賢思齊焉見不賢而內自

由察 子曰士父母幾諫 幾猶剴諫父母者剴切之禮子士父有隱無犯也 見志不從又

而無違勞而無怨孝子父母在無所自專鄉[illegible]

長道而已子曰父母在不遠遊遊必有 之由常處 子曰

於之道可謂孝意 孝子哀慕不改其父之弟道非心所忍為也 子曰父母之年

則以懼 見其壽考則喜見其衰老則懼 子曰故者言之不出恥躬之不逮 [illegible]

及仁之言不忘出口為身行將不及之 子曰以約失之者鮮矣 約儉之者恆足[illegible] 子曰君子

訥於言而敏於行 言欲難行欲疾 子曰得不孤必有鄰

則德來德相達 子游曰士君斯辱矣朋友數斯疏矣 之曲

論語公冶長第五 孔氏本 鄭氏注

子謂公冶長可妻也雖在縲紲之中非其罪以其子妻之

公冶長孔子弟子縲紲徵點之屬所以執縛罪人之繩索冶長嘗以他仁之罪為執法吏所拘制時仁或辱之孔子憐之

有道不廢邦無道免於刑戮以其兄之子妻之

益德之子男容悅之字一名韜也 子謂子賤君子哉若仁 子賤孔子弟子宓不齊之字若仁[illegible]

CHAPTER TWO

On Seeking Knowledge

Never feel contented in study and teach others tirelessly.

Confucius always asked himself this question: "Keep in mind what I have learned, study hard, and teach others tirelessly. Have I done all these things?"

Quick, and eager to learn. Modest, and never ashamed of asking questions.

Confucius' disciple Zi Gong asked why someone was given the honorary title "Wen" (cultured). Confucius answered: "Because he was bright and ready to learn. He never felt ashamed to learn from those who were of lower status or less educated than him."

If one learns the truth in the morning, one can never regret dying in the evening.

During the reign of Emperor Zhu Run (1399-1402) in the Ming Dynasty, a man named Yang Fu successfully passed the imperial examinations, and became an official in charge of recording and compiling the dynasty's history. Later, he was charged with a crime and imprisoned for 10 years. During his imprisonment his food rations were suspended several times, and he nearly starved to death. However, Yang Fu never stopped studying. His fellow inmates mocked him: "What's the use of study in such a place?" Yang Fu smiled and said: "If I learn the truth in the morning, I will not regret dying in the evening."

One studies so diligently that he forgets his meals and so happily that he forgets his worries, and is even unaware of approaching old age.

Ye Gong, a senior official of the State of Chu, asked Zi Lu what kind of person Confucius was, and Zi Lu didn't answer. Confucius later asked Zi Lu: "Why didn't you answer his question? You should have said: 'Confucius studies so diligently that he always forgets his meals and so happily that he forgets his worries, and is even unaware of approaching old age.'"

When walking with other people, there is always someone from whom one can learn a great deal. Find their merits and discover their shortcomings. Learn from their merits and study their shortcomings to help overcome one's own shortcomings.

During the Spring and Autumn Period a man in the State of Wei was curious about how Confucius acquired his knowledge, and went to ask Zi Gong, who said: "My teacher learns everywhere and from everyone. He does not follow a particular instructor." Confucius later said: "While walking with other people, there must be one I can learn from. I shall pick out their merits to follow and spot their shortcomings for reference to overcome my own shortcomings." This was just what Confucius did in life. He had ever consulted the duke of the State of Tan on ancient official rites, consulted Chang Hong, senior official of the State of Eastern Zhou, on ancient music, and learned how to play music from Shi Xiang, the official in charge of music in the State of Lu.

If one doesn't study when he is young, he will be of no use when he grows up.

Confucius taught his disciples: "A gentleman has to examine himself in three situations: if he doesn't study in youth, he will be incapable when he grows up; if he doesn't give guidance to his children and grandchildren, he will not be missed after death; if he is reluctant to donate when he is rich, he cannot expect help when he is needy. Therefore, one should think of one's future when one is young, and thus study hard, think of matters after death when one is old, and thus instruct one's children and grandchildren; and think of the bitterness of poverty when one is rich, and thus dedicate oneself to charity."

To be capable, one must study; to be intellectual, one must learn from others.

General Wen Zi of the State of Wei asked Zi Gong: "I heard that Confucius is dedicated to civilization by way of education. He first taught his disciples poems and literature, then gave a speech on filial piety, respect for elders and benevolence, and made them witness rituals and ceremonies. In this way he guided them toward a high moral standing. Some 70 of his disciples are now accomplished in learning. Who among them are sages?" Zi Gong said he didn't know. Wen Zi asked: "You study together. And you are a sage yourself. How could you say you don't know?" Zi Gong answered: "It is difficult to know the sage, because they won't crow about themselves. That's why the gentleman says that nothing requires more wisdom than learning from others. Wen Zi said: "Though it is difficult to know the sage, you are studying with Confucius now. So I ventured to ask you this question." Zi Gong replied: "Confucius has some 3,000 disciples. Some of them study with me during the same period of time, some don't. Therefore I cannot name each disciple. According to Confucius, to be capable, one must study; to be intelligent, one must learn from others."

If one can acquire new knowledge by reviewing old knowledge, one is qualified to be a tutor.

Confucius often discussed with his disciples on how to study and how to become a teacher. One day a disciple asked what was most important for study and what are the qualifications for becoming a teacher, to which Confucius answered: "A person in pursuit of knowledge should always review what one has learned. In this process one can gain new insight. This is most important for further study. If one can acquire new knowledge by reviewing old knowledge, one is qualified to be a tutor."

If I give a student one example and he cannot draw inferences from it, then I will teach no further.

Initially, Confucius had great political ambitions. But his political views were not accepted by China's rulers. He thus turned to writing and teaching in a bid to promote his political and philosophic ideas. Confucius had a set of teaching theories and methods. For instance, he once said "If a student doesn't have a strong desire to learn, his study cannot see much progress despite his tutor's effort." He also said: "If I give a student one example and he cannot draw inferences about others from it, I will not teach him any more."

When a person is absent-minded, he can't see with open eyes, can't hear with ears, nor even taste while eating.

One day Confucius discussed with his disciples the topic of correcting thought and cultivating moral character. A disciple asked: "Why must one correct one's thought before cultivating moral character?" Confucius answered: "Because the heart guides the body. When one's heart is filled with anger, joy, or worry, he cannot straighten up his mind. As the body is a medium for the mind to express itself, if one cannot correct one's thought, how can one correct one's behavior?" Confucius later offered further explanations on the relationship between correcting thought and cultivating moral character: "When one is inattentive, one cannot see anything with open eyes, cannot hear with both ears, and knows nothing of taste, even while eating. Color, sound, and taste are the simplest things to learn. If an absent-minded person cannot distinguish these, he can in no way discern the subtle connotations of axioms. How can people correct their thinking in pursuit of morality?"

CHAPTER THREE

On Honesty and Credibility

Always stand by one's words, and persist in one's undertaking till the end.

Zi Gong was eager to learn, and always raised questions without hesitation. One day he saw the character Shi (gentleman). At first he thought he understood its meaning, but upon further introspection he discovered he knew the "how's" but not the "why's" about the meaning of Shi. He thus went to ask Confucius what kind of person can be called a gentleman. Confucius thought a moment and replied: "There are three grades of gentlemen. Those of the first grade restrain themselves with sense of honor, and accomplish the tasks consigned by the emperor during their official visit to foreign states." Zi Gong asked: "How about gentlemen of the second grade?" Confucius said: "They are praised by family member for filial piety, and lauded by townsmen for respect to the elders." Zi Gong asked again: "What about gentlemen of the third grade?" Confucius answered: "These people always stand by their words and persist in their undertaking till the end." Zi Gong was thus inspired by Confucius' instruction.

S peak with trustworthiness and act with honesty and conscience.

Confucius' disciple Zi Zhang asked how he could bring success to everything he did. Confucius said: "If one speaks with trustworthiness and acts with honesty and conscience, one can get things done anywhere in the world. If not, he cannot make any achievement even in his hometown. While one is standing, one should see these words as if they were in front of your eyes. Whenever you are traveling, you should see these words as if they were carved in the hillside. If you can keep this in mind, you can always succeed everywhere." Thereafter, Zi Zhang wrote this sentence on his belt so he could see it constantly.

How can a person behave himself if he cannot keep his word?

One day Confucius was talking with a few disciples. One of them asked: "I've heard that credibility is the cardinal principle of conducting oneself in society. Is it true?" Confucius replied: "How can one be acceptable without being trustworthy in words? This is just like a cart without a collar-bar or a carriage without a yoke. How can they move forward? This is the way to behave oneself. Without credibility, one has no restraint."

One cannot find a place in society until he is courteous, honest, and loyal.

Yan Hui was traveling to the western regions, and asked Confucius about the principle of conducting oneself. Confucius said: "One can only find a place in society and evade misfortune by being courteous, honest, and loyal. If you are respectful to others, they will protect you; if you are loyal to others, they will help you; if you are credible to others, they will rely on you. When people protect, help and rely on you, you can not only avoid disasters, but prevent them. If one cares only about one's appearance rather than one's soul and moral character, does one thus go in the wrong direction? If one doesn't consider or prepare for the difficult times until they occur, isn't it too late?

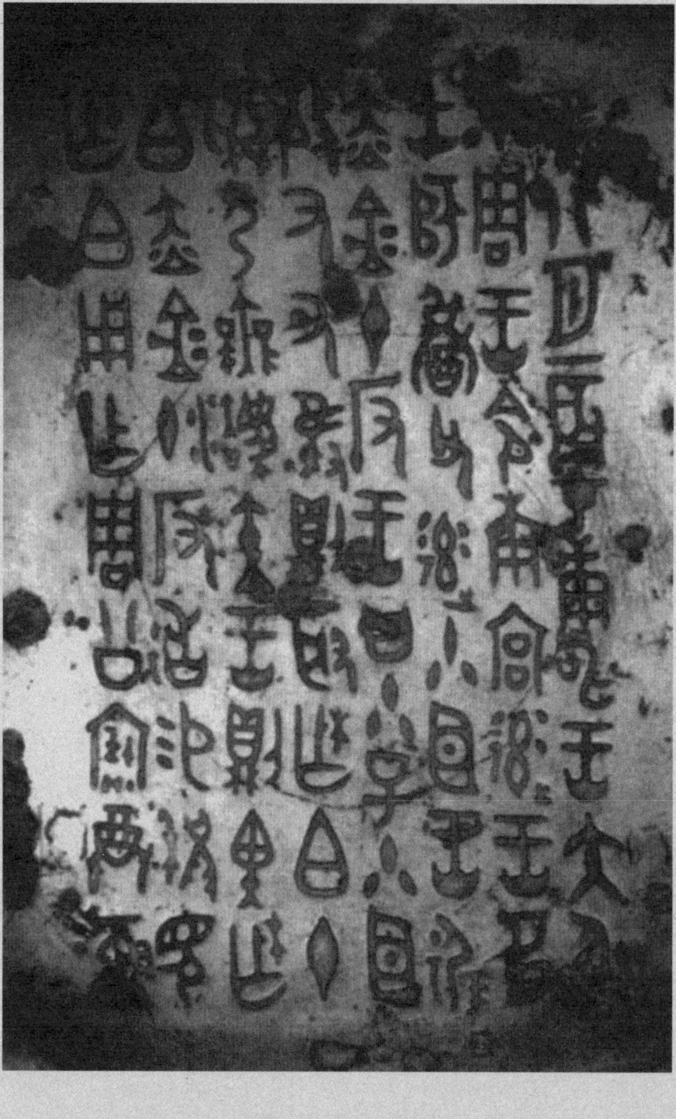

CHAPTER FOUR

On Being Modest

Though being capable and well learned, one should ask those less capable or learned for advice.

Zeng Shen and Yan Hui, both disciples of Confucius, were good friends. After Yan Hui died, Zeng Shen often recalled the days they studied together with admiration of his friend's learning and moral standing. Zeng Shen said: "Though being capable and well learned, he asked those less capable or learned for advice. Though being erudite and intelligent, he presented himself with modesty."

One who thinks himself wise cannot hear any good advice.

Confucius sighed when he read the chapter on gain and loss in the *I Ching*, or, *The Book of Changes*. His disciple Zi Xia, who was sitting nearby, asked: "Why do you sigh, Master?" Confucius replied: "People gain to lose, and lose to gain. That's why I sigh." Zi Xia asked: "Do we not gain through study?" Confucius said: "I don't mean the gaining of knowledge. Scholars gain knowledge at the cost of health. They take a humble attitude towards others' advice, and therefore can have great learning. So, one who thinks himself wise cannot hear any good advice."

Gentlemen speak with behavior, petty men speak with their tongues.

One day Yan Hui asked Confucius: "What's the difference in how a gentleman and a petty man speak? Confucius replied: "Gentlemen speak with their behavior; petty men speak with their tongues. Gentlemen may dispute one another on matters concerning the pursuit of justice, but are respectful of each other in other issues; petty men have the same interest as long as they are making trouble, but resent each other the rest of time."

One who talks too much is prone to failure.

On several occasions Confucius and his disciples journeyed to various regions across China. One day they arrived in the former capital of the Zhou Dynasty and visited its ancestral temple. There was a bronze figure in front of the main hall of the temple, whose mouth was covered over with cloth strips. The disciples were confused. Confucius told them: "This is an ancestor who was prudent in speech." Confucius was then reminded of his defeat in seeking an official position, and lamented: "Ancient people were so cautious about their words; we should learn a lesson from them. Never speak too much. One who talks too much is prone to failure." It is said that these words were later inscribed onto the back of the statue.

Don't explain what has been done; don't advise on what has been finished; and don't reprehend that which has already taken place.

Duke Ai of the State of Lu asked Zai Yu: "Why were different trees used while offering sacrifice to the God of Land in previous dynasties?" Zai Yu answered: "Ancient people planted trees while offering sacrifice to the God of Land. Pines were planted in the Xia Dynasty, cypresses in the Yin Dynasty, and chestnuts in the Zhou Dynasty. The Zhou Dynasty chose the chestnut because it sounds like the word for "fear" and would prevent people from opposing them." Confucius heard of this and was angry at Zai Yu's imprudence. He said: "Don't explain what has been done; don't advise on what has been finished; and don't reprehend that which has already taken place."

That which is most believable is what one sees, but one can't always trust his eyes. That which is most reliable is what one thinks, but one can't always trust his brain.

During his travels, Confucius was delayed in the States of Chen and Cai, and was without food for many days. One day Yan Hui found some rice and cooked it. When the rice was almost done, Confucius noticed that Yan took a small bit of rice and ate it. Even though Confucius saw this, he did not say anything. When Yan Hui invited Confucius to eat, Confucius said: "I have just dreamed of my father. The clean food should be offered to him as sacrifice." Yan Hui said: "Some soot fell in the rice moments ago. It would be a pity to throw the whole pot away, so I picked out the contaminated rice and ate it. Since I have eaten some of the rice, the rest is not clean anymore, and therefore cannot be offered as sacrifice." Confucius regretted questioning Yan Hui's honesty, and sighed, "That which is most believable is what one sees, but one can't always trust his eyes. That which is most reliable is what one thinks, but one can't always trust his brain. Disciples, you should remember how difficult it is to know a person."

CHAPTER FIVE

On Correcting
Mistakes

Not to correct the mistake one has made is to err indeed.

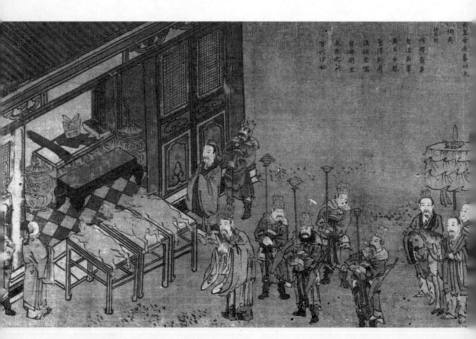

At the end of Western Zhou Dynasty (c.1100-771 B.C.) Emperor Li was ruthless and tyrannical, arousing resent among the people. He was furious that people would dare complain about him, and gave the order to execute all who criticized him. Duke Zhao suggested him not to do this, saying: "It is more terrible to gag the people than to block the river." But the emperor wouldn't listen. Later the people rose up and Emperor Li was overthrown.

Never be afraid of correcting mistakes one has made.

Yuan Ran was Confucius' old friend. When Yuan's mother died, Confucius helped him with the coffin. Zi Lu said: "You have always told us: 'don't make friends with those not so good as you, and never be afraid of correcting mistakes you have made.'" Confucius replied: "We should help whoever in difficulty, not just an old friend." When the coffin was finished, Yuan Ran was so happy that he sang. Confucius felt sad, but pretended he didn't hear his song. Zi Lu complained: "You condescended to help him, while he was so impolite to you." Confucius said: "It's said that family is family, and friend is friend." Confucius was ever tolerant of others.

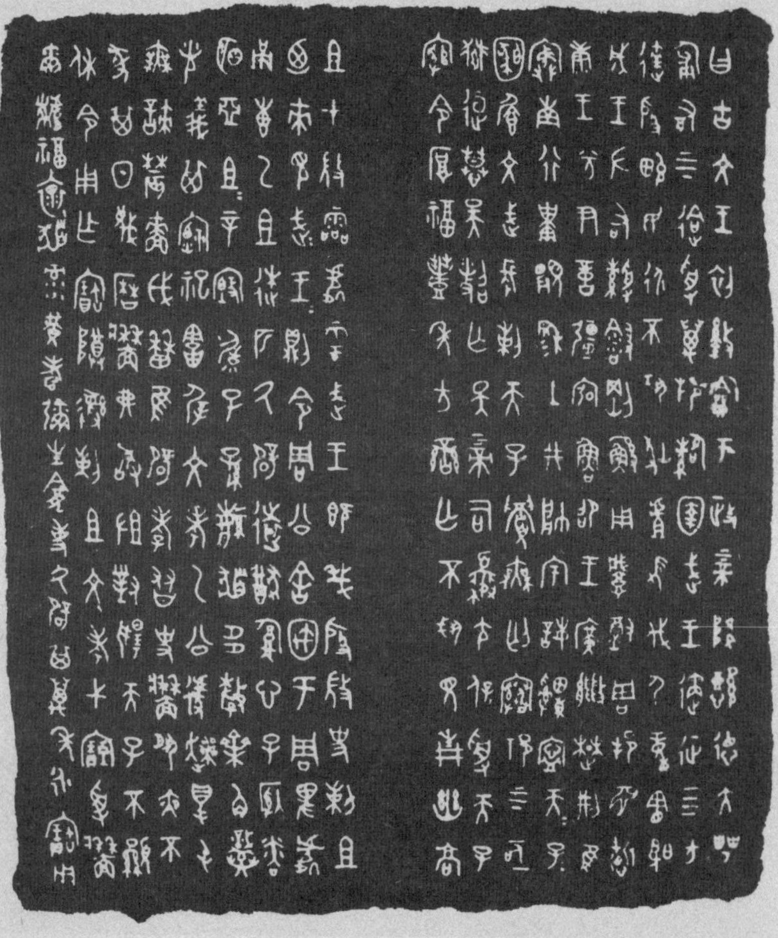

CHAPTER SIX

On Being Filial

When the tree wants to stop swaying, the wind keeps blowing; when children want to fulfill filial duty to parents, the parents have passed away.

One day while walking with some disciples Confucius heard someone crying. He went forward, and saw Gao Yu, in coarse clothes and with a sword in hand, wailing miserably. Confucius asked him what was the matter. Gao Yu replied, weeping uncontrollably: "I have made three mistakes: When I was young, I was eager to learn, so I traveled far and wide and didn't take care of my parents before they died. This was my first mistake. Holding high and noble goals, I didn't serve the emperor, so I have accomplished nothing. This was my second mistake. I had many close friends, but as the years passed I severed ties with them, so I have no one to rely on when I am old. This was my third mistake. The tree may crave calm, but the wind won't stop; when the children want to fulfill their filial duty, their parents have passed away. Time passes and never returns. Parents pass away and can never come back. I feel so much regret now. Let me die." Gao Yu then cried himself to death. Confucius stood in silence and told his accompanying disciples: "You should draw a lesson from him, and keep it in mind." Afterward, thirteen of his disciples left Confucius to return home and serve their parents.

When one's parents are alive, one should not go far away from home. If one has to, one should tell them where one is going.

Confucius always told his disciples to give consideration to their parents' feelings. One of his disciples was to take a position in another part of the country, but hesitated when thinking of his elderly parents. He asked Confucius for advice. Confucius said: "When one's parents are alive, one should not go far away from home. If one has to, one should tell them where one is going, so that parents can call one back whenever necessary." The disciple took this advice. He accepted the appointment, but also informed his parents of where he would be.

One who walks a long way with a heavy load is not picky about the place where he rests; one who is poor and has old parents to support should not be choosy about an official position, whether it is well paid or not.

Zi Lu was very respectful to his parents. Later he recalled: "One who goes a long way carrying a heavy load is not picky about the place where he rests; One who is poor and has old parents should not reject official appointment even if it does not pay well. When my parents were alive, I ate coarse food and saved my rice for them. I walked many miles to bring the rice home, and felt happy despite of all the hardship. After my parents passed away, I made a trip to the State of Chu to assume my position. In my entourage were hundreds of carts carrying tremendous amount of grain. I was deeply sad, for I knew that never again would I be able to carry rice to my parents."

Run away when father flogs with a big stick; take the beating when the stick is small.

Zeng Shen once made a mistake, and for it his father beat him almost to the point of unconsciousness. When his father had finished, Zeng rose to his feet and asked: "Are you still angry, father?" People praised Zeng for showing filial piety, but Confucius told his disciples: "Don't let Zeng Shen in when he comes." Zeng didn't think he did anything wrong, but Confucius said: "Haven't you ever heard of Shun, the legendary sage king? When his father wielded a small stick, he took the beating. When his father tried to flog him with a big stick, he ran away. When his father had work for him to do, he was always beside his father, but when the old man wanted to kill him in a fury, he could never be found. You didn't leave when your father got so angry. What if he killed you in a moment of rage? He would have been accused of cruelty, and that is the least filial way of looking at the situation.

CHAPTER SEVEN

On Making Friends

至聖先師孔子 名丘字仲尼山

東兗州府曲阜縣人

Keep your promises to friends.

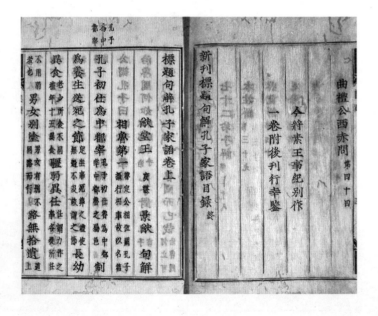

During the Eastern Han Dynasty (25-220 A.D.) Zhang Shao and Fan Shi studied together in the capital city of Luoyang, where they became good friends. On their departure, Fan promised to visit Zhang in two years. On the promised date Fan arrived, travel-worn and weary. Zhang had already prepared his home and received his friend warmly.

T ake delight in advertising others' merits and in making virtuous friends.

Confucius said: "There are three kinds of beneficial pursuits and three kinds of harmful pursuits. Enjoy a moderate amount of food and music, praise other people's merits, and make many virtuous friends. These are all beneficial pursuits. To be arrogant about one's position, to be lax or idle, and to indulge overly in food and drink are harmful pursuits."

It is beneficial to make friends with those who are upright, honest and erudite. It is harmful to make friends with those who are crooked, boastful, and flattering.

One day Confucius talked with his disciples about the criteria of selecting friends. He believed that making the right friend was most important when one was in school. According to Confucius, there are three kinds of people one should make friends with, and three kinds of people one shouldn't. It is beneficial to make friends with those who are upright, honest and erudite. It is harmful to make friends with those who are crooked, boastful, and flattering.

To make friendship last one should purposely stress friends' merits and avoid exposing their demerits.

It was a rainy day and Confucius was going out, but he could not find an umbrella. One of his disciples said: "We can borrow one from disciple Pu Shang." Confucius replied: "He is stingy about his money and possessions. I heard that to make friendship last one should purposely stress one's friends' merits and avoid exposing their demerits." Confucius chose not to borrow an umbrella from Pu Shang for fear of exposing his shortcomings.

If one has learnt the truth but doesn't put it into action, it is better not to learn at all. If one is close to others but doesn't trust them, it is better not to be close to them at all.

Confucius' elder brother Kong Mie consulted Confucius on how to behave oneself in society. Confucius said: "If one has learnt the truth but doesn't put it into action, it is better not to learn at all. If one is close to others but doesn't trust them, it is better not to be close to them at all. Never be overwhelmed when something good happens or too anxious when something bad happens." Kong Mie asked: "So what should I do?" Confucius replied: "Try to overcome your shortcomings, and to achieve the ability you don't have as yet. Don't suspect others when you have faults, nor look down upon others when you have talents. Don't say or do anything that others can hold against you. Only the wise people can do all these things."

A gentleman should be cautious in deciding whom he will follow. If he follows someone bad, the result can be as disastrous as that of a bird flying towards a net.

Confucius saw a man catch birds with a net, and noticed all the birds he had captured were young birds. He asked: "why can't you catch adult birds?" The man answered: "Young birds that follow adult birds cannot be captured; adult birds that follow young birds can be captured." Confucius turned to his disciples and said: "A gentleman should be careful about selecting the person he follows. If one follows someone bad, the result can be as disastrous as a bird flying towards a net."

Associating with good people is like living in a room full of orchids; associating with bad people is like living in a salted fish store. After a while neither smell is noticeable.

Confucius told his disciples: "After my death Zi Xia's knowledge will increase, while Zi Gong's will decrease." Zeng Shen asked why. Confucius said: "Zi Xia prefers to get along with people who are wiser than him, while Zi Gong prefers to get along with people who are less wise than him. If you don't know the son, look at his father; if you don't know a person, look at his friends; if you don't know the emperor, look at his officials; if you don't know the soil, look at the grass that grows on it.

Give earnest advice to friends, but stop doing so if they won't follow.

One day Zi Gong consulted Confucius on making friends. Confucius said: "When friends make mistakes, one should give them earnest advice. But one should stop doing so if they won't listen.

Gentlemen unite instead of conspiring; petty men conspire instead of uniting.

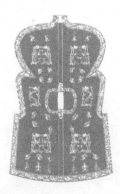

Zi Gong asked Confucius: "All people admire gentlemen, and want to be like them. But who can be called gentlemen?" Confucius replied: "A gentleman puts his idea into action before speaking. Gentlemen are different from petty men. The difference lies in whether they are honest and righteous in dealing with affairs and people, and draw a clear distinction between public and private interests. Gentlemen unite instead of conspiring; petty men conspire instead of uniting."

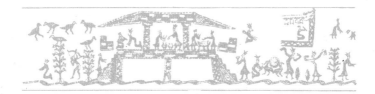

CHAPTER EIGHT

On Conducting Oneself in Society

周禮卷第九

秋官司寇第五　　　鄭氏注

惟王建國辨方正位體國經野設官分職

以為民極乃立秋官司寇使帥其屬而掌

邦禁以佐王刑邦國　禁所以防姦者也刑正人之法孝經說曰刑者侀也

罪施　過出　刑官之屬大司寇卿一人小司寇中

大夫二人士師下大夫四人鄉士上士八

人中士有六人旅下士三十有二人　士察

A gentleman aids others in doing good deeds, but never aids them in bad deeds. A petty man does the opposite.

Zi Zhang consulted Confucius on politics. Confucius said: "While helping people, one should help them with patience through to the end, and follow up on what he has said. A gentleman aids others in good deeds, but never aids them in bad deeds. A pretty man does the opposite."

A gentleman gives help to the needy not to the wealthy.

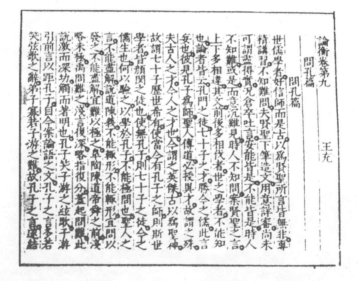

Disciple Ran You asked Confucius for some grain to give to the mother of Hu Gongxi, another disciple, who had been called away on business for a long period of time. Confucius said: "Give her 64 bushels" Ran You asked for more, Confucius said: "Give her 24 bushels more. Ran You thought it was still not enough. He took some rice of his own and gave a total of 80 bushels to the old woman. Confucius, however, criticized him by not being able to judging wealth properly. Confucius said: "When Hu Gongxi departed, he was dressed in a light fur coat and rode a fine horse. He doesn't need much help. A gentle-man gives help to the needy but not the wealthy."

A gentleman is free from worries and fears.

Sima Niu asked what he should do in order to be a gentleman. Confucius answered: "A gentleman is free from worries and fears." Sima Niu asked: "Is a man called a gentleman when he is free from worries and fears?" Confucius replied: "If a gentleman thinks introspectively and always has a clear conscience, how can he feel worry or fear?"

When impoverished, gentlemen persevere in their virtue while petty men act in defiance of it.

Confucius and his disciples ran out of food during their travels in the State of Chen. They were so starved that they could not even walk. Zi Lu looked sullen, and asked: "Can gentlemen become impoverished?" Confucius answered: "When impoverished, gentlemen persevere in their virtue, while petty men act in defiance of it."

One should help others do what one desires to do himself and achieve what one desires to achieve himself.

Zi Gong asked Confucius: "What do you think of a man who brings broad benefits to the people? Is he benevolent?" Confucius said: "Far more than being benevolent, he must be one of the greatest of all sages. To be benevolent is to help others establish what one desires to establish himself and achieve what one desires to achieve himself. To put oneself in the shoes of others is the way to benevolence."

Be rigorous on crucial issues of ethics. Lapses on minor issues of ethics are allowed.

On his way to the State of Tan, Confucius met Cheng Zi, and the two engaged in hearty talk for the entire day. At the end of their meeting Confucius turned to Zi Lu and said: "Bring a bundle of silk for Master Cheng." Zi Lu said nothing. Later Confucius repeated: "Bring a bundle of silk for Master Cheng." Zi Lu replied coldly: "I was told a gentleman never meets strangers without introduction of the intermediary, nor marries a girl without help of the matchmaker." Confucius said: "The Book of Songs reads: 'In the field where dew glitters on the grass I met a pretty girl. If I don't take the chance to give her a gift, I may never see her again.' One should be rigorous on crucial issues of ethics, but lapses on minor issues of ethics are allowed."

One who loves people is loved by others; one who despises people is despised by others.

Duke Ling of the State of Wei asked Confucius: "I was told that one can rule the state if he is prudent with his words and behavior. Is it true?" Confucius replied: "Yes. If you love others, they will love you; if you despise others, they will despise you. Since you know how to treat yourself, you should know how to treat others. One can know of great events around the world without leaving one's small residence, for one is aware of self-examination."

CHAPTER NINE

On Rule

To rule is to be just and upright. If the ruler is just and honest, how could others not follow his example?

Ji Kangzi, an official of the State of Lu, consulted Confucius on the rule of the state. Confucius said: "To rule is to be just and upright. If you are just and honest, how could others not follow your example?"

The most important thing about rule is to win the support of the people.

Duke Ai of the State of Lu consulted Confucius on how to run the country. Confucius said: "The policies of Emperor Wen and Emperor Wu of the Zhou Dynasty (1100-771 B.C.) are still recorded on bamboo strips. When an emperor is on the throne, his policies are implemented; when he is no longer on the throne, his policies are no longer implemented. The rule of heaven lies in the creation of lives; the rule of people lies in hard work concerning state affairs, and the rule of earth lies in plants and animals. Just as rain and dew are crucial to the growing of plants, support of the people is the most important factor toward the rule of a country."

One who knows how to be an official abides by the law and does good deeds; one who doesn't know how to be an official does the opposite.

Zi Gong was appointed magistrate of Xinyang County, and came to Confucius to say goodbye before he left. Confucius told him: "Be diligent in official business, and act according to the will of the people. Never take by force, assault by words, tyrannize, or pillage. Zi Gong asked: "I have been following you since I was very young, but never has such a thing happened. What is meant by your words?" Confucius said: "Assault is to condemn those more talented and virtuous; tyrannize is to stifle the search for truth by summoning the executioner; pillage is to take others' credit for oneself. Does pillage only mean robbery of money? I heard that one who knows how to be an official abides by the law and does good; one who doesn't know how to be an official does the opposite. This is the source of hatred."

One who is good at being an official contracts grace, one who isn't contracts hatred.

An official of the State of Wei, Ji Gao, once sentenced a man to have his foot cut off for a serious crime. Years later, after a riot hit the state, Ji Gao tried to flee the city. At the city gate he encountered the gatekeeper, and was shocked to see that the man had only one foot. The gatekeeper told Ji Gao: "There is a gap in the wall over there." Ji Gao replied: "A gentleman never climbs across the wall." The gatekeeper then suggested: "There is a hole in the wall over there." Ji Gao replied: "A gentleman never climbs into a hole." The gatekeeper said at last: "Here is an empty house. Take refuge there." Ji Gao entered the house and escaped the mob running after him. When all was clear, Ji Gao asked the gatekeeper: "You knew it was I who gave the order to cut off your foot? Why did you help me when I was in danger rather than take revenge?" The gatekeeper replied: "I deserved my punishment. When you announced the verdict, I saw the sadness in your face and knew you were kind and sympathetic. So I helped you escape." Confucius heard of this story and said: One who is good at being an official contracts grace, one who isn't contracts hatred. Only those like Ji Gao can make just decisions."

Set a good example for the subordinates, forgive their minor mistakes, and promote the talented.

Zhong Gong was selected to be an aide of a senior official in the State of Lu, and asked Confucius how to deal with government affairs. Confucius said: "Set a good example for your subordinates, forgive their minor mistakes, and promote those who are talented." Zhong Gong asked: "How can I find the talented to promote them?" Confucius replied, "First, select the talented who you already know. For those who you don't know, watch how they learn and select them."

Judge a horse by watching it draw the cart, judge a person by watching his everyday behavior.

In the State of Lu during the Spring and Autumn Period, Zi Yu, a man with an unpleasant appearance, applied to be one of Confucius' disciples. Confucius at first worried he was not a good person, but agreed at last with reluctance. Later Confucius could see that Zi Yu was a kind, intelligent, and thoughtful person, and many people wanted to be taught by him. Confucius said, "I almost missed Zi Yu by judging him only by his appearance."

Govern the people with the greatest care as if driving a galloping horse with a broken rein.

Zi Gong consulted Confucius on how to govern the people. Confucius said: "Be cautious as if you are driving a horse with a broken rein." Zi Gong said: "How horrible that would be!" Confucius replied: "The population is large in the country where transportation is convenient. Guided properly, they are as submissive as your pet; if not, they are all your foes."

When the righteous people are promoted and evil people are dismissed, the public will obey; If not, they will disobey.

Duke Ai ruled the State of Lu at the end of the Spring and Autumn Period, when power struggles were rampant. In a situation where powerful states bullied weak states, the duke went to Confucius for advice on how to govern the country. He asked: "What should I do to convince my people?" Confucius replied: "If you promote righteous people and dismiss evil people, the public will obey; if you do the opposite, they will disobey."

Make the people rich first, and then educated. This is essential to rule of a state.

Prince Liu De of the Han Dynasty once commented: "The people cannot appreciate rites until their barns are filled with grain, and cannot know honor or disgrace until they have sufficient food and clothing. When there are plentiful provisions, the country is powerful, women are graceful, rites are implemented and the public is content. According to the Documents of the Elder, affluence ranks first among the five happinesses, the others being longevity, good health, good moral character and dying naturally and peacefully." Confucius told Zi Lu: "Make the people rich first and then educate them. This is the crucial to rule of a country."

CHAPTER TEN

On Philosophy

Going too far is as bad as not going far enough.

Confucius' disciple Zi Gong asked: "Whom do you think is better, Zi Zhang or Zi Xia?" Confucius replied: "Zi Zhang always overdoes it, while Zi Xia doesn't do enough." Zi Gong asked: "Do you mean that Zi Zhang is better?" Confucius replied, "Going too far is as bad as going not far enough."

By accepting others' advice, one can become a sage.

Confucius and Zi Lu were deep in discussion one day. Confucius said, "If an emperor doesn't have officials who are willing to offer suggestions, his rule will be corrupt; if a gentleman doesn't have friends who can admonish him, his moral character will be corrupt. By accepting others' advice, one can become a sage. If one is dedicated to study and does according to what one learns, how can one not be successful? If one abandons benevolence and faith, and abhors the traditions of a gentleman, one is doomed to punishment." Zi Lu retorted: "Bamboo grows straight without being trimmed. Cut and made into arrows, they can pierce the hide of a rhinoceros. How can this be the result of study?" Confucius replied: "Can not the arrow go deeper into the target if its tail is decked with feathers and its point is sharpened?" Zi Lu realized the point of the lesson and laughed heartily.

Aking can't become a real ruler without encountering difficulties; one who values faith and justice more than life can't become outstanding without facing adversity.

Confucius and his disciples traveled to the State of Chu on the invitation of Duke Zhao. Upon hearing this news, officials of the states of Chen and Cai met and conspired: "Confucius is a sage. If he takes a senior post in the State of Chu, our states will be in danger." So they sent troops to block Confucius' way. After being out of food for seven days, all his disciples were dejected, but Confucius kept reciting poems, playing music, and singing as usual. Zi Lu asked: "Does it conform with the rites to sing under such conditions?" Confucius said: "The suffering is blessing to me and to you as well. I was told that a king can't become a real ruler without encountering difficulties; one who values faith and justice more than life can't become outstanding without facing adversity."

One who has his arms broken three times may become a good doctor.

When Confucius and his disciples finally resumed their trip, his disciples sighed: "We can never forget this suffering." Confucius said: "What nonsense! Have you never heard of the saying that one who has his arms broken three times may become a good doctor? This suffering is a blessing to us. I was told that a king can't become a real ruler without encountering difficulties; and soldiers can't become crack troops without suffering setbacks."

Rotten wood cannot be carved, nor can a wall of dried dung be whitewashed.

Zai Yu was the most disliked among Confucius' disciples. He once proposed to discuss with his master the merits of the five ancient emperors (Huang Di, Zhuan Xu, Di Ku, Tang Yao and Yu Shun). Confucius refused sternly: "You are not qualified." One day Confucius saw Zai Yu sleep during the daytime, and said: "The rotten wood cannot be carved, nor can a wall of dried dung be whitewashed. Since Zai Yu is so slothful, I don't see any use to scold him."

If one doesn't have the right status, what he says is not justifiable; when his words are not justifiable, what he does can't be successful.

Zi Lu asked Confucius: "What are you going to do first if you are invited to come to the State of Wei?" At that time in the State of Wei there was great upheaval amid a brutal contest for power between the duke and his sons. Confucius replied: "I will rectify the status of the people first." Zi Lu said, "How can you be so pedantic? Why do you haste to rectify the status of the people?" Confucius replied: "A gentleman must be prudent about what he does not know. I have my reason to rectify the status of the people first. When one is not in the right status, what he says is not justifiable; when his words are not justifiable, what he does can't be successful."

Abstruse knowledge can be transmitted to those whose talent is above average, but never to those whose talent is below average.

One day Confucius discussed education with his disciples. Some disciples said that the most important role of education is to make clear the explanation of various theories. Some disciples argued that a good explanation is in vain if the student cannot comprehend the basic elements of a theory. Other students believed that explanations could be made to clever people but not to foolish people. Confucius thought that all their opinions were somewhat one-sided, saying: "Teaching should be conducted in light of the students' talent. Most people in the world are of average talent. Abstruse knowledge can be transmitted to those whose talent is above average, but never to those whose talent is below average."

Fragrant and smelly grass cannot be stored in the same vessel; Yao (an ancient wise emperor) and Jie (an ancient tyrannical ruler) cannot rule a country together.

During a trip with his disciples Zi Lu, Zi Gong, and Yan Hui, Confucius asked them about their aspirations. Zi Lu blurted: "I wish I could lead an army to occupy a land that stretches for 1,000 li, take the enemy whole, and cut off the soldier's ears as a record of my heroic deeds." Zi Gong said: "If a war breaks out between the states of Qi and Chu, I will persuade them to reach a truce." Yan Hui didn't say anything. Confucius asked him: "Don't you have any aspiration?" Yan Hui replied: "They have talked about both military and civil ambitions, what else can I say?" Urged by Confucius repeatedly, Yan Hui said at last: "Fragrant and smelly grass cannot be stored in the same vessel. My aspiration is to assist a wise emperor to bring peace and affluence to the county and people." Confucius sighed: "How lofty Yan Hui's moral character is!"

CHAPTER ELEVEN

On Everyday Life

Good preparation secures success. Poor preparation leads to failure.

Duke Ai of the State of Lu consulted Confucius on politics: "What are the principles of ruling a state? How does the ruler carry them out?" Confucius replied: "Whatever one does, he should make good preparation or he will fail. It is like that one should work out a draft in mind before speaking so that he will not speak wrongly. Preparation should be made before action is taken to avoid setback. Research should be made before a policy is implemented. One should think before acting or speaking. Only by doing so he can expect success."

A craftsman must prepare his tools beforehand in order to do his work well.

Zi Gong asked how to practice benevolence. Confucius said: "A craftsman must prepare his tools beforehand in order to do his work well. In order to practice benevolence in a country, one should serve the virtuous officials and make friends with benevolent gentlemen."

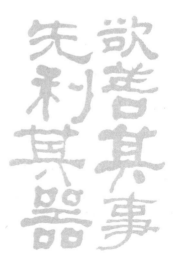

The moral character of a gentleman is like the wind, while that of a petty man is like grass.

Ji Kangzi consulted Confucius on the ruling of a country: "What do you think of governing a country by killing villains and being close to good people?" Confucius said: "Why must you kill to rule? If you want to do good, your subjects will do good. The moral character of a gentleman is like wind, while that of a petty man is like grass. The grass bends to whichever direction the wind blows."

Never make haste, nor covet small gains. Eager for quick success, one may not reach his goals; Covetous of small gains, one cannot make great achievements.

Before taking office of magistrate of Jufu County, Zi Xia asked Confucius for advice on government. Confucius replied: Never make haste, nor covet small gains. Eager for quick success, one may not reach his goals; Covetous of small gains, one cannot make great achievements.

When the water is too clear, the fish cannot live in it; When one is too stern, no one can make friends with him.

Shen Linshi, a renowned scholar of Southern Qi Dynasty (479-503), was very amiable. Once his neighbor lost his shoes, and suspected that Shen's shoes were in fact his. Shen then gave his shoes to his neighbor, smiling. The neighbor later found his own shoes, and returned Shen's shoes. But Shen didn't blame him at all. Shen was widely appraised for his affability.

If one doesn't have a strict regimen, does not practice moderation in eating and drinking, or lives life either too simply or in too complicated a manner, he will expect bad health or even death.

Duke Ai of the State of Lu asked Confucius: "Do all those who are wise and benevolent enjoy longevity?" "Yes." Confucius replied. "There are three causes of death. But the dead can blame nobody but themselves. If one does not practice moderation, he will die of illness. If one is in a lower position, but offends his seniors, or is too rapacious, he will die of punishment. If one affronts those more powerful and influential, or isn't aware of his limitations, he will die in war. Those who are wise and benevolent can restrain themselves. They know what they should do and what not, when they can be happy and when they can be angry. They never run counter to the laws of nature. How could they not live a long life?"

Notes to Illustrations

p3. Portrait of Confucius.

p4. *Zilu Asking Confucius* (detail).

p6. Auspicious door couplets.

p7. Portrait of Empress Wu Zetian.

p9. Bronze urn. Originally a cooking vessel, it later became a symbol of power.

p10. Painting of an orchid by Zheng Sixiao, and kept by Qing Emperor Jiaqing.

p16. Patterns on vessel fragments during the Spring and Autumn and Warring States periods.

p20. *The Analects*. Tang Dynasty edition.

p23. *Confucius Teaching* (detail).

p24. *Confucius in the Journey*.

p26. A Confucian lecture.

p31. *Qiao Yuan Loves Three Things*.

p36. *Confucius Asking about Rites*.

p38. Portrait of Confucius, painted by Ma Yuan and kept in the Museum of the Imperial Palace.

p39. Thatched cottage built by Zi Gong in memory of his teacher, Confucius.

p40. *Stone Pavilion* (detail) by Cai Jia of Qing Dynasty.

p42. *Jiaping Stone Sutras* (detail).

p46. Bronze tripod with iron feet of King Zhongshan, Warring States Period.

p49. Details of the painting *Confucius Retired to Compose Poems and Write Books*.

p115. Portrait of Zi Gong.

p118. Bronze wine vessel of the Western Zhou, unearthed in Shaanxi in 1976.

p121. Pages of *Zhou Rites* of Song edition.

p122. Bronze lamp of the Warring States Period, unearthed at Zhucheng, Shandong, in 1957.

p124. *Asking Confucius* by Wang Chong.

p126. Bronze lamp in the tomb of King Zhongshan.

p136. Ceremonial tripod from the Spring and Autumn Period.

p139. Embroidery with dragon and tiger patterns of the Warring States Period.

p141. Bronze urn.

p148. Statute of Confucius in the Confucius Temple of Nanjing.

p149. Gilded tripod in cloud pattern of the Spring and Autumn and Warring States periods, unearthed in Xianyang, Shaanxi Province.

p160. Bronze sacrificial vessel of the Western Zhou, unearthed in Liaoning Province in 1955.

p163. Ruins of city wall, State of Lu.

p172. Green jade pendant in the shape of a seated figure.

p178. Bronze helmet unearthed from a Shang tomb at Xingan, Jiangxi, 1989.

p180. Bronze bird-shaped ceremonial vessel of the Western Zhou.

p183. A stone tablet at a Confucius Temple.

p190. Jade dragon, unearthed at Chifeng, Inner Mongolia.

p191. Ming Dynasty landscape, Liaoning Province.

p195. A stone tablet with the image of Confucius teaching.